970L

Biography®

Daring PIRATE WOMEN

Anne Wallace Sharp

A&E®

Lerner Publications Company
Minneapolis

Lerner Publications Company
A division of Lerner Publishing Group
241 First Avenue North
Minneapolis, MN 55401 U.S.A.

Website address: www.lernerbooks.com

Library of Congress Cataloging-in-Publication Data

Sharp, Anne W.
    Daring pirate women / by Anne W. Sharp.
        p.   cm. — (A&E biography)
    Includes bibliographical references and index.
    Summary: Profiles pirates throughout history, especially women pirates of Europe, America, and Asia, such as Princess Alvilda, Ingean Ruadh, Grany Imallye, Elizabeth Killigrew, Anne Bonny, and Lai Cho San.
    ISBN: 0–8225–0031–0 (lib.bdg. : alk. paper)
        1. Women pirates—Biography—Juvenile literature. [1. Pirates.
    2. Women—Biography.] I. Title. II. Biography (Lerner Publications Company).
    G535.S52   2002
    910.4'5—dc21
                                                            00–008908

Manufactured in the United States of America
1 2 3 4 5 6 – JR – 07 06 05 04 03 02

CONTENTS

*In the early 1700s, many pirates plied the waters around
Charleston, South Carolina.*

Chapter **ONE**

DREAMS OF ADVENTURE

THIRTEEN-YEAR-OLD **A**NNE **C**ORMAC YEARNED TO RUN away and find a more exciting life. Born in Ireland, Anne had moved to South Carolina with her parents in the early 1700s. According to legend, a chance encounter in Charles Towne (present-day Charleston) only increased her desire for adventure.

Although there is no historical evidence, the popular legend says that Anne and her father, William Cormac, went to Charles Towne to purchase supplies for their plantation. They were beginning to shop when Anne's father pulled her into an alleyway. He pointed across the street, urging her to be quiet. She saw a huge man dressed all in black. A shiver ran up her spine.

Her father whispered that the man was none other

than the infamous pirate Blackbeard. Anne couldn't take her eyes off him, feeling that he could see her even though she was well hidden in the shadows. His black eyes gleamed as he swaggered, bigger than life, into a tavern across the way.

In that brief encounter, Anne took in everything she could about the pirate's appearance. His beard alone was of mythic size, hanging down below his waist. His hair, fixed in tiny pigtails, was decorated with dozens of bright red ribbons. She also noticed that he was heavily armed. He must have had at least six pistols in the belt that lay across his chest. And his shiny cutlass (a short sword) nearly dragged on the ground.

Anne could hear him roar with laughter inside the tavern, and the sound made her blood run cold. But, oh, how she wanted to meet him and hear his tales of pirating.

Anne had heard that before a battle, Blackbeard tried to look as evil as possible. She had also heard that most enemy captains feared him so much that they surrendered to him without a fight. Once she had seen Blackbeard for herself, Anne didn't doubt this for a minute.

As she and her father returned home, young Anne smiled to herself. Someday, she knew, she would meet a real pirate and sail away with him.

And that's just what Anne did. She married the pirate James Bonny and became a pirate herself. Soon she was living a life filled with danger, adventure, and crime.

Blackbeard was one of the most infamous pirates in the Americas.

BLACKBEARD—TERROR OF THE ATLANTIC

f all the pirates who ever sailed the seas, the most famous was Edward Teach, known as Blackbeard. For several years in the early 1700s, he sailed along the east coast of North America, terrorizing everyone who crossed his path.

Dressed in black and always heavily armed, Blackbeard looked evil. To make himself look even more terrifying, the pirate put slow-burning fuses under the brim of his hat. When set afire, these fuses gave off smoke that encircled Blackbeard's head.

Blackbeard ruled his ships with an iron fist. On one occasion, he shot his first mate in the knee during a card game, leaving the man with a permanent limp. This kind of violence kept his pirates frightened and under his control. During the years that Blackbeard ruled the seas, "both victims and fellow pirates believed him to be the Devil."

Blackbeard died as he had lived—violently. His end came in 1718, when British naval lieutenant Robert Maynard caught up with him off the coast of North Carolina. After a lengthy battle at sea, the pirate died of numerous wounds and was then beheaded. Legend has it that on nights when the moon is full, Blackbeard's body can be seen swimming in the North Carolina waters, looking for his severed head.

Edward Teach, or Blackbeard, opposite page, was known on the high seas as a ruthless and powerful pirate. Many people feared him due to his reputation and his menacing appearance.

Pirates—Fact and Fiction

Pirates. The word itself captures our imagination. Their names—Captain Kidd, Blackbeard, Calico Jack—and their deeds have been told time and time again.

Pirates are often portrayed in books and film as romantic figures. Tales of swashbuckling pirates engaged in masterful swordplay have long fascinated young and old alike. The stories are filled with daring adventures, chests filled with glittering gold and silver, and deserted tropical islands where fortunes still lie buried. Perhaps the most famous fictional pirate comes from Robert Louis Stevenson's classic book *Treasure Island*. The book is about a map, some buried treasure, and an uprising aboard a ship led by the colorful pirate Long John Silver, a one-legged rascal with a parrot on his shoulder.

Despite such romantic stories, real pirates were criminals. They were sailors who raided other ships and port cities. Most pirates robbed merchant vessels, especially those carrying gold, silver, and other precious goods. In addition to stealing a ship's cargo, pirates sometimes seized the ship and its crew, or sunk the ship and killed the crew. Many pirates were navy or merchant seaman who mutinied—took control of their ships by force and then turned to pirating.

When merchant ships were captured, sunk, or destroyed, great fortunes were lost. The groups that owned the ships and their cargoes—shipping

Robert Louis Stevenson's Treasure Island *(published in 1883) paints a romantic picture of pirate life featuring Long John Silver,* above.

When captured, pirates were usually hanged, and their bodies were left as a warning for other criminals.

companies, businesses, and governments—all lost vast amounts of money. Because they disrupted trade, pirates were considered enemies to civilized society. They were among the most detested of all criminals and were hunted down and killed all over the world. The punishment for "robbery on the high seas" was nearly always public execution by hanging. In many locations, pirates were left strung up for days or even weeks as a message and warning to pirates and desperadoes everywhere.

It is difficult to write histories about pirates. There are few accurate books about them. And because they risked being hanged for their crimes, pirates did not keep diaries or logs that tell of their deeds. In many cases, trial records are the only sources of information about some pirates. These documents usually consist only of trial verdicts and dates of execution. Because of the lack of books and records, historians have a hard time separating fact from fiction when it comes to pirates.

Perhaps the most-used source on piracy is *The General History of the Robberies and Murders of the Most Notorious Pyrates,* written by Charles Johnson and published in London in 1724. Johnson's book was based on hundreds of interviews he conducted with real pirates, as well as newspaper stories and government reports. Unfortunately, Johnson included several fictional biographies in his book and, at times, added imaginary conversations. Modern scholars doubt the accuracy of many of Johnson's stories.

PIRATES THROUGH HISTORY

Throughout history, piracy has been widespread in many parts of the world. The first documented report of piracy comes from ancient Sumer, located in present-day Iraq. Around 3000 B.C., pirate crews sailed up the Tigris and Euphrates Rivers and attacked the Sumerians. These pirates hurt Sumerian trade for many years until the Sumerians eventually defeated them.

From the late 700s to about 1100 A.D., Viking pirates terrorized much of Europe. The Barbary Coast pirates, raiders from the north coast of Africa, attacked ships and cities in the Mediterranean region from 1400 to 1800. Throughout much of the last thousand years, Chinese pirates, sailing in fast boats called junks, raided much larger vessels in the South China Sea.

Piracy reached a peak in the Caribbean Sea and Atlantic Ocean during the late 1600s and early 1700s. The Spanish had discovered gold and silver in Mexico and South America, and Spanish fleets filled with treasure regularly sailed from the New World back to Europe. Other Europeans followed the Spanish, setting up colonies and businesses in North, South, and Central America. Merchant ships filled with valuable cargoes sailed back and forth across the Atlantic.

Pirates came from all over the world to prey on these ships. In North America, every port city was home to at least one pirate crew, while many large towns had entire communities of pirates. This "Golden Age of Piracy" lasted from approximately 1650 to 1725. It included many of the most notorious pirates, such as Blackbeard. In the early 1700s, the British government began to crack down on piracy in its New World colonies. Many pirates were executed, and others were promised pardons if they would give up pirating. Blackbeard was killed by a British naval officer in 1718, and the Golden Age ended soon afterward.

Blackbeard, right, *was finally defeated by Robert Maynard,* left, *in 1718. Blackbeard's head was hung from the bowsprit of a ship as a symbol of his fate.*

Boys aboard ship often wore baggy clothing and long hair, left. So it was possible for women to sneak onto ships disguised as boys.

WOMEN AND THE SEA

On the whole, pirating was a man's job. After all, women's lives were very restricted in earlier eras. Up until the late 1900s, most women were expected to stay home and raise children. They were excluded from many jobs, including sailing. Occasionally, captains' wives accompanied their husbands aboard ship. In China whole families sometimes lived and worked at sea. But in Europe and the Americas, sailing ships were primarily male territory. Most sailors believed that women couldn't tolerate the physical demands of a seagoing life. Many sailors believed that a woman on a ship was likely to provoke jealousy and conflict among the crew. Finally, sailors felt that a woman at sea would bring the ship bad luck and disaster.

Despite such attitudes, some women did manage to go to sea. A few of them even became pirates. Most women had to disguise themselves as men to become sailors and pirates—they would not have been allowed onboard ship otherwise.

Female pirates stood far apart from the more conventional women of their time. Rather than leading traditional lives at home, they chose lives of adventure—and crime. From the waters of the North Atlantic to the Caribbean to the South China Sea, they sailed vessels and raided other ships. Most of these women are not included in modern history books or even anthologies about piracy. But, in many countries, their legends live on. And their stories make fascinating reading.

The Vikings were fierce Scandinavian pirates who thrived during the Middle Ages.

Chapter **TWO**

THREE VIKING PRINCESSES

FOR MORE THAN FOUR HUNDRED YEARS, THE VIKINGS
took the world by storm. In search of land, gold, silver,
and slaves, these warriors and explorers from Norway,
Sweden, and Denmark ruled the seas. They were
shrewd traders, excellent navigators, superb ship-
builders, and fearsome pirates. The speed of their boats
and their daring were legendary. The word *Viking*
comes from "Vik," the name of a pirate center in southern Norway. Among Scandinavians, the expression "to
go a-viking" means to fight as a pirate or warrior.

Using classic pirate tactics of terror and surprise, the
Vikings spread fear from the 700s well into the 1100s.
They raided ships throughout Europe, voyaged as far
as Baghdad in the Middle East, and even reached

parts of North America. In addition to raiding vessels at sea, the Vikings also traveled inland on rivers. Meeting little resistance, they overran large cities and small towns alike. They often demanded huge payments in exchange for leaving an area in peace. Then, in their boats filled with riches, the Vikings sailed victoriously home.

Viking men were famous for being courageous and bold, and Viking women are remembered for being totally independent. While the men were at sea, many Viking women managed farms, raised children, and ran households single-handedly. But some Viking women went to sea themselves, and several have earned a place in Viking folklore.

PRINCESS ALVILDA

The most dramatic tale of a female pirate of the Viking era is the story of Princess Alvilda—also known as Alwilda or Altilda. She sailed in the North Atlantic Ocean during the 1100s. Several historians have written about her adventures. The first was the twelfth-century historian Saxo Grammaticus. The details of her story read like a fairy tale, however, and modern historians aren't sure how much of the tale is true.

Alvilda was the daughter of the Swedish king Sypardus. According to the story, Sypardus was so jealous of his daughter's many suitors that he kept her locked up in a high tower and had her guarded by poisonous snakes. The king said that anyone who wanted his

Legends tell of Alvilda's great pirating adventures.

daughter's hand in marriage would first have to kill the snakes and climb the tower.

Many men tried to kill the poisonous snakes but all failed, many of them dying in the process. One day a young man named Alf, the son of the king of Denmark, came to try his luck against the snakes. He successfully killed them and stormed into the tower, only to find that Alvilda was gone. Her mother had helped her escape and had provided her with a ship. Alf was furious and swore to pursue Alvilda to the ends of the earth.

The princess recruited an all-female crew, made up of her serving maids and the women of her court. They soon became pirates, plundering and raiding merchant ships. Alvilda's career got a real boost when she encountered another pirate vessel that had recently lost its captain. Alvilda assumed command of the ship, with its crew of seasoned male pirates.

Alvilda's raids were hurting Danish business. The king decreed that this pirate must be stopped. He sent the Danish fleet, led by his son Alf, to capture the pirate. But Alf had no idea that the pirate he was pursuing was a woman—much less the one he had once hoped to marry.

Alf found Alvilda on the seas near Finland. The Danish fleet surrounded her ship. Although Alf was victorious in the battle that followed, he lost some of his best warriors and ships. He swore revenge on the pirate who had inflicted such heavy losses.

Alf ordered the pirate captain brought to him. Dressed for combat in armor and a helmet, the pirate appeared before the prince. The pirate did not flinch as Alf approached, sword in hand. Alf reached over and knocked off the pirate's helmet. He gasped when a thick mass of red hair fell about the pirate's shoulders. According to the tale, Alf promptly proposed marriage.

PRINCESS SELA

Princess Sela was another Viking pirate. Her brother was Kolles, the Norwegian king. Historians know that Sela really existed. But, as with Alvilda, they don't know how much of her story is true.

Stories say that Sela and Kolles hated each other. Whether the reason was a simple rivalry between sister and brother or something more, we shall probably never know. We do know that when Kolles became king, his sister went to sea and became a pirate. In her quest for riches, she attacked every ship that crossed her path in the North Atlantic Ocean.

Sela led daring raids. She amassed quite a reputation and a substantial treasure. Perhaps she should have been satisfied with her growing wealth. However, her hatred for her brother intensified. She was bitterly determined to defeat him.

Kolles was also a pirate—always in search of more wealth, power, and territory. His greed led to his own end, and his sister's.

VIKING SHIPS AND WEAPONS

Viking warships were masterpieces of construction and seaworthiness. Called longships, they carried Viking warriors across wild and turbulent seas. Carvings of ferocious animals, gods, and goddesses adorned these boats and terrified enemies. If these carvings weren't sufficiently frightening, the Vikings also dyed their sails blood red.

The average longship was more than seventy-five feet long and was steered by a large oar attached to the boat near the stern. The ships were fast and flexible and could cruise up narrow channels with ease. On the open seas, Viking sailors raised a

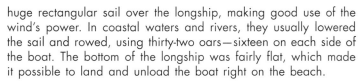

huge rectangular sail over the longship, making good use of the wind's power. In coastal waters and rivers, they usually lowered the sail and rowed, using thirty-two oars—sixteen on each side of the boat. The bottom of the longship was fairly flat, which made it possible to land and unload the boat right on the beach.

Each vessel carried up to fifty warriors, who wore helmets of leather or iron and carried stout round wooden shields, painted with bright colors. Their weapons were swords, spears, and powerful axes, all made of iron with wooden handles. The ax, the Viking's most common weapon, was usually four to five feet long. The spear had a long shaft fitted with an iron spearhead. A good sword was a Viking warrior's most prized possession. It was often decorated with gold and silver.

A reconstructed Viking ship and a modern-era crew dressed as Vikings

He and his crew set off to attack a small island off the coast of Norway. When Sela heard of his plans, she quickly pursued him. She arrived too late, finding him already dead at the hands of an enemy. By then, Sela had sailed into danger as well. In the ensuing battle with her brother's killer, the princess also met her death—or so the story goes.

THE RED MAIDEN

Another Norwegian princess also had a tragic conflict with her brother. She was Ingean Ruadh, also known as Rusla, or the Red Maiden. Like Alvilda and Sela, Rusla definitely existed and is documented in Viking history. How much of her story is true, however, we do not know.

According to the story, Rusla and her sister Stikla were pirates. For many years, they raided ships and cities in Iceland, Denmark, and the British Isles. It was Rusla's conflict with her brother, King Tesondus of Norway, however, that consumed her. Tesondus had lost his crown to the Danish king. Disgusted with her brother's failure, Rusla decided to avenge his loss by sending her own fleet to wage war on the Danes. If Tesondus couldn't defeat them, then she would.

Not long afterward, she chanced upon her brother's ship and sank it. In the aftermath of the battle, her brother was able to swim safely to shore. Rusla debated whether or not to pursue and kill

Rock carvings in Sweden show images of Viking longships.

him. She decided to let him go. She sailed away and continued her attacks, terrorizing the coastlines of many countries.

Tesondus was determined not only to regain his crown but also to get revenge. With a number of ships, he set out to capture his sister. With his own ship in the lead, he eventually found her and attacked. In the ensuing battle, her ship was capsized. Rusla was captured and brought before her brother.

If she was expecting Tesondus to be lenient because she had once allowed him to escape, she was mistaken. Tesondus came swaggering up to her and "ordered that she be beaten to death with the oars." The Viking princess was killed, but her legend lives on.

Irish pirate Grace O'Malley, left, *pleads with Queen Elizabeth I,* right, *to release her brother and son from prison.*

Chapter **THREE**

PIRATES OF THE BRITISH ISLES

IN **1577** ENGLISH HISTORIAN SIR HENRY SIDNEY wrote about a famous Irish pirate: "There came to me also a most feminine sea-captain called Grany Imallye . . . with three galleys [ships] and two hundred fighting men. . . . This was a notorious woman in all the coasts of Ireland."

Grany Imallye, whose Gaelic name is Grace O'Malley in English, was a notorious pirate. (Gaelic is the historic language of Ireland, and, with English, one of its two official languages.) Thanks to numerous references in the state papers of Ireland, we know that she existed. Recent research has also uncovered many of the main events of her life. So it is with documented proof that we can write of Grace O'Malley and her life of piracy.

O'Malley was born around 1530 into a seafaring family. Her father was a local chieftain in Connaught on the western coast of Ireland. For centuries, his family had ruled the area around Clew Bay. The O'Malleys had numerous castles in the area, but their greatest claim to fame was at sea. The O'Malley clan ran a legitimate shipping business, but they also practiced piracy on the side.

Grace was her father's favorite child. She was at home aboard ship and shared her father's love of the sea. Her father taught her the fine points of sailing. She quickly became "one of the boys" and had her hair cut short to fit in. This haircut gave rise to the nickname that would follow Grace her entire life— Granuaile, which means "bald one" in Gaelic.

During this era, England was trying to take control of Ireland. In 1541 English king Henry VIII declared himself to be the king of Ireland as well as England. The O'Malleys refused to recognize Henry's claim on their nation. They made war on English vessels in the seas around Ireland.

In one encounter with the English, Grace's father told her to hide below deck. Instead, she climbed into the rigging of the sails. Watching the battle from above, she saw an English sailor sneaking up behind her father with a dagger. Grace leaped off the rigging onto the sailor's back, screaming and creating a distraction. This uproar allowed Grace's father to regain control of the ship and defeat the English.

Resisting the authority of King Henry VIII of England, above,
Grace and the O'Malleys attacked English vessels.

Queen Elizabeth I tried to strengthen English rule throughout Ireland.

At age sixteen, Grace married a neighboring clan leader, Donal O'Flaherty. They eventually had three children. In this era, Irish leaders often fought among themselves for land and titles. Donal was killed defending an island he had captured.

After Donal's death, Grace and her three children returned home to her family. Then her father died, and she assumed control of the vast O'Malley empire. Her brothers offered no objections, for their father had trained Grace well for this role. Those who met her described her as a gracious and charming woman with a twinkle in her eyes. Charming or not, she was a pirate through and through.

In 1558 Elizabeth I became queen of England. Elizabeth tried to strengthen English control in Ireland. She sent English noblemen and soldiers to rule Irish territory. In many areas of Ireland, these rulers passed unpopular laws and often enforced them with violence. In Connaught where Grace lived, this rule was particularly harsh.

To make matters worse, local chieftains continued to fight among themselves for control of the counties and territories of Ireland. Many of these chieftains made war against the O'Malleys. In return, Grace led punishing raids against other Irish leaders while continuing to attack and plunder passing English vessels.

The Irish coast was a perfect place to practice piracy. The coastline includes a large number of bays that pirate ships could use as safe hiding places.

Grace knew the coastline well and used it to her advantage. In addition to attacking passing ships, she and her pirates also patrolled the coasts, charging ships huge fees for the use of "her" waters. Taking advantage of the brisk sea trade between England and Spain, Grace was able to amass quite a fortune.

Grace was so successful, in fact, that Queen Elizabeth put a large monetary reward on her head. The queen ordered her Irish governor to send troops against Grace, but they were repelled at her castle. The queen briefly considered sending in the royal fleet but decided

WAITING FOR GRACE O'MALLEY

owth Castle sits on the Irish coastline, just north of Dublin. Legend has it that Grace O'Malley once stopped at this great house and asked for lodging and food on her long way home from England. The lord of the castle, perhaps afraid of being robbed, refused to let her enter.

Possessed of a fiery temper, Grace sought revenge by kidnapping the lord's son. Her terms of settlement were simple. In exchange for his son, the lord had to promise to make Howth Castle more hospitable in the future. He was asked to set the table for Grace at every meal thereafter. Some say that the current owner of Howth Castle still keeps this promise.

not to. She feared that her sailors would suffer defeat and humiliation at Grace O'Malley's hand.

In 1566 Grace remarried—this time to chieftain Richard Burke, nicknamed Iron Richard. Richard lived at Rockfleet Castle, overlooking Clew Bay. On this windswept area of the Irish coast, tremendous gales and storms made the water choppy and gray. With the complete support of her husband, Grace kept a fleet of twenty pirate vessels anchored there. From this base, she led raids against neighboring chieftains and passing cargo ships.

Because Grace continued to capture and rob their ships, local merchants raised a storm of protest against her. In March 1574, the English government again tried to stop her. An English force sailed into Clew Bay and attacked Rockfleet Castle. Grace's pirates easily defeated them.

The English finally captured Grace O'Malley in 1577. A government official, Lord Justice Drury, noted that "Grany O'Mayle [Grace O'Malley], a woman that hath impudently passed the part of womanhood and been a great spoiler, and chief commander and director of thieves and murderers at sea ... having been apprehended ... his Lordship hath now sent her to Lymrick where she remains in safe keeping." She was eventually released as part of a hostage exchange between the English and the Irish.

Once released, Grace and her pirate fleet continued to attack ships off the Irish coast. Around 1590, nearly sixty

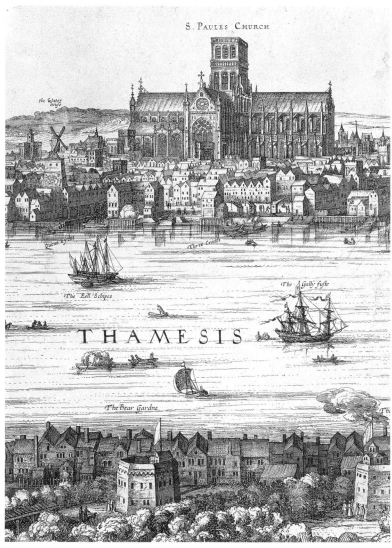

Grace wrote to Queen Elizabeth in London, which lies along the banks of the Thames River, above.

years old, Grace led her fleet against a Spanish ship. Usually leaving the hand-to-hand combat to her men, Grace became concerned when the advantage seemed to be swinging toward the Spaniards. Coming on deck in her nightgown, Grace stormed into the fray. Carrying a sword in one hand and a pistol in the other, she began yelling and screaming curses at the enemy. Legend has it that the Spanish immediately dropped their weapons and surrendered.

Not long afterward, Iron Richard died, leaving Grace in a predicament. According to Irish law of the time, a widow could not inherit her husband's property. Grace refused to give up Rockfleet Castle and set out on a series of new raids. These attacks brought a fast response from the English government, which sent out the royal fleet. This time, the English were successful and captured several O'Malley ships, as well as Grace's brother. Grace felt that the only thing she could do was appeal to Queen Elizabeth.

In a letter to the queen, Grace asked for the release of her brother. She begged for protection from her enemies and enough money to support her in old age. In return, she promised to stop attacking English ships and to make her fleet available to the queen during times of war. Grace wrote: "In tender consideration... and in regard of her great age, she most humbly beseeches your majesty of your princely bounty... to grant her some reasonable maintenance for the little time she has to live." She went on to ask the queen "to grant unto your said subject . . . free liberty during her life to invade with sword and fire all your highness' enemies."

While the queen's advisers were considering the pirate's request, Grace learned that her son had been arrested on charges of inciting a rebellion. He had led a mob that had attacked some government buildings. In September 1593, with her son facing execution, Grace went to London to appeal to the queen in person.

The queen decided to give the Irish pirate an audience. As Grace entered the royal chambers, she reportedly walked proudly toward the queen and shook her hand with vigor. An old poem recalls the scene:

> 'Twas not her garb that caught the gazer's eye—
> Tho' strange, t'was rich and after its fashion
>   good—
> But the wild grandeur of her mien erect and
>   high.
> Before the English Queen she dauntless stood,
> And none her bearing there could scorn as rude;
> She seemed as one well used to power—one that
>   hath
> Dominion over men of savage mood,
> And dared the tempest in its midnight wrath,
> And thro' opposing billows cleft her fearless path.
>
> And courteous greeting Elizabeth them pays,
> And bids her welcome to her English land

And humble hall. Each looked with curious gaze
Upon the other's face, and felt they stand
Before a spirit like their own. Her hand
The stranger raised—and pointing where all pale
Thro' the high casement, cam the sunlight bland,
Gilding the scene and group with rich avail;
Thus to the English Sov'reign, spoke proud
  Grana Wale [Grace O'Malley].

Grace stated her case. No one knows exactly why, but Queen Elizabeth granted all of the pirate's requests. Grace's brother and son were released from prison. Grace was allowed to keep her fleet and pursue her former pirate activities—but this time on behalf of the English. She lived out the rest of her years as an English privateer—a pirate who operates against enemy ships with government permission. She died in 1603 at Rockfleet Castle and was buried on Clare Island near her home. Years after her death, her deeds were remembered in song:

'Twas a proud and stately castle in the years of
  long ago,
When the dauntless Grace O'Malley ruled a
  queen in fair Mayo.
And from Bernham's lofty summit to the waves
  of Galway Bay,
And from Castlebar to Ballintra her unconquered
  flag held sway.

WOMEN OF THE HIGH SEAS

Various women in the British Isles and in France operated as pirates on the high seas. Below are short biographical descriptions of three of these historic pirate women:

Jane de Belleville: Jane de Belleville, who lived in the 1300s, was a French noblewoman. The French executed her husband, charging that he was an English spy. Enraged, Jane sought revenge on the French. She sold her jewels and bought and outfitted three pirate ships. Then she cruised along the coast of France, attacking French vessels and burning down French villages.

Charlotte de Berry: Born in England in 1636, Charlotte de Berry grew up dreaming of a life at sea. By dressing as a man, she followed her husband into the Royal Navy. Their ship was eventually captured by a pirate ship headed toward Africa. The pirates gave the naval crew two choices: become pirates or be killed. Most sailors, of course, including Charlotte, chose the first option. Life with the pirates was not pleasant for Charlotte, whose identity as a woman was discovered not long after her

ENGLAND'S LADY KILLIGREW

From Cornwall, the southwesternmost county in England, comes the story of the infamous pirate Lady Elizabeth Killigrew, who also lived during the 1500s. The Killigrews, a well-respected clan led by Sir John Killigrew, owned Arwenack Castle. The family had ship was captured. Shortly thereafter, the ship's captain assaulted her. Taking advantage of the other pirates' dislike of the captain, she encouraged the crew members to mutiny. In the fight that ensued, Charlotte cut off the captain's head with a dagger. Then Charlotte took command of the vessel. For many years, she and her crew sailed along the African coast, capturing ships filled with gold. Historians are unsure about how and where Charlotte met her death.

Maria Lindsay: One of the most bloodthirsty of all sixteenth-century English pirates, male or female, was Maria Lindsay of Plymouth. She once tied up the captain and first mate of a captured ship and used them for target practice, reportedly firing eight different pistols at them one after another. Another time, Maria and her husband captured a British naval vessel. She so admired one of the officer's uniforms that she had him strip out of his clothing. As she laughed at the young man, Maria calmly killed him with her sword. From that time on, she wore his uniform constantly. During yet another capture, Maria and her husband took over a merchant vessel off the coast of Scotland. The survivors were put in leg irons and were then served a supper that Maria had prepared: poisoned stew. The men all died within an hour.

more than its share of politicians, musicians, and soldiers. But the Killigrews were also pirates.

John Killigrew and his wife, Elizabeth, led a rich and adventurous life. He was in charge of the family business, which included not only seizing ships but also hiding and selling stolen goods and boats. The

Elizabeth Killigrew was a lady of high standing— and a ruthless pirate.

Killigrews paid substantial fees to harbor and city officials, bribing the officials to look the other way when crimes were committed.

Elizabeth played an active role in all Killigrew activities and apparently loved the thrill of piracy even more than her husband did. She had learned the pirate trade from her father. Over the years, she became quite a sailor and businesswoman.

On one occasion, in 1582, a large Spanish ship entered the harbor and docked near Arwenack Castle. A violent storm developed. While the Spanish crew stayed onboard ship, the ship's captain and first mate decided to sit out the wind and rain in the warmth and comfort of the castle. The two men received the best of English hospitality there. Lady Killigrew brought them food and drink and made them feel quite at home. The men were so content in the luxurious surroundings that they delayed their departure for a few days.

What the two men didn't know was that Lady Killigrew and her husband, while entertaining their visitors, were also quietly checking out the vessel anchored in their harbor. It was a valuable boat whose cargo would add riches to their already massive family fortune.

Leaving her Spanish visitors to relax, Lady Killigrew led her pirate crew through a secret tunnel from the castle down to the sea. With the storm still raging, she and her pirates rowed silently out to the great ship. Lady Killigrew led the rowboats closer and closer, until her men were able to climb up and board the vessel. Taking the guards completely by surprise, the pirates killed everyone on board and threw their bodies into the sea.

After filling their rowboats with the ship's cargo and treasure, Lady Killigrew and her crew returned to the castle. Hiding the loot in yet another secret passageway, she simply changed clothes and returned to entertaining. While she and her husband sat again with the captain and first mate, several of her pirates sailed the great Spanish ship out to sea and sank it. The entire venture took less than two hours.

When the rains finally let up, the Spanish sailors returned to their ship—only to find that it had completely disappeared, crew and all. Their suspicions naturally fell on Lady Killigrew and her husband. It was impossible, however, to prove that a crime had been committed—since all the evidence had vanished without a trace.

Elizabeth, the English queen, preferred to overlook the Killigrews' acts of piracy. She knew she could rely on the family to act as her privateers in time of war. As long as the Killigrews did not prey on the queen's friends, they were free to pursue their pirate ways.

Later in 1582, the Killigrews made a near-fatal mistake. A rich German merchant ship was anchored in Falmouth Harbor, close to Arwenack Castle. Although English and German leaders had close ties, the Killigrews couldn't resist the temptation to go for the gold. Lady Elizabeth selected a small band of her best fighters and crept alongside the ship under the darkness of night. Within a matter of minutes, the German ship was hers—and the sailors on board had been killed and thrown overboard.

Queen Elizabeth was furious. She immediately had the Killigrews arrested. Lady Killigrew was sentenced to death, but at the last minute, the queen pardoned her. Apparently, the queen did not want to make permanent enemies of the powerful Killigrew family. The lady was quickly released.

Little is known about Lady Killigrew or her husband after this episode. Most historians suspect that she and her family simply continued their various businesses after her release from prison. She died a few years later.

Galleons such as the one pictured above were typical merchant ships during piracy's Golden Age.

Chapter FOUR

ANNE BONNY, MARY READ, AND THE GOLDEN AGE OF PIRACY

PIRACY FLOURISHED IN THE AMERICAS FROM ABOUT 1650 to 1725. This was the Golden Age of Piracy, when the seas were filled with ships of every kind and pirates of every description. Pirate captains such as Blackbeard became legends. As in earlier eras, some women became pirates too.

What caused such a flurry of piracy? The answer begins with Spain's seizure of many New World territories in the 1500s. The Spanish found vast amounts of silver and other precious resources in Central and South America. Seizing the wealth from the native peoples, the Spanish began to ship it back to Spain by way of the Caribbean Sea and the Atlantic Ocean. The value of the cargoes excited many people's imaginations.

Soon, other Europeans arrived to exploit the riches of the New World. In the 1600s, England, France, and other European nations set up colonies in the Americas. Ships filled with a variety of expensive cargo sailed back and forth across the Atlantic Ocean. As trade in the Americas grew, the number of pirates there grew as well.

BECOMING A PIRATE

The reasons people became pirates in the 1600s and 1700s are complex. A mix of social and economic factors came into play. Some may have been attracted to the thrills of a dangerous, wild life, but many sailors who turned to piracy never set out to be pirates at all. In fact, most pirates began life as honest seamen on board merchant or naval ships.

In Europe and North America, boys commonly became sailors as teenagers, or even younger. Their first jobs usually involved providing gunpowder to the gunners, so they were called "powder monkeys." Later, these boys would assist older seamen, who taught them all the basics of ship life: handling the sails, steering, navigating, stowing cargo, and maintaining the vessel.

Because life at sea was difficult and often dangerous, crew members frequently quit the job. Many others were injured or killed at sea. Often shorthanded, naval captains were always on the watch for new recruits.

Many sailors went to sea during childhood. They usually started out as powder monkeys, running gunpowder to sailors manning the ship's cannons.

Despite popular images of victims walking the plank, this kind of punishment is probably just a myth.

When they couldn't find volunteers, captains some-times sent groups of men ashore to round up new sailors in any way they could. Called press-gangs, these men used any number of tactics to get men aboard ship. They often kidnapped unsuspecting vic-tims. They also tricked men into service by getting them drunk. When the victim sobered up after a long night of drinking, he found himself on ship and far out to sea.

Whether they came onboard willingly or were pressed into service, all sailors faced hardships aboard ship. The food was usually poor, the work was dan-gerous, the pay was low, and the discipline was often harsh. Consequently, if their ships were captured by pirates, many seamen chose to become pirates them-selves. Some crews didn't wait for a pirate attack. They simply mutinied. They took control of their ships by force, often killing the captain, and set out as pirates themselves.

On most pirate ships, sailors had to agree to a strict code of conduct. This code usually included rules on how treasures were to be divided and on specific pun-ishments for crimes. Crimes of murder, stealing, and de-sertion were tried in a pirate's court, with a jury of pirates and the captain as the judge. Although books and movies often show victims being forced to walk the plank, there is no record of this punishment really oc-curring. Instead, a sailor found guilty of a serious crime was either thrown overboard or executed by a firing squad. But what pirates feared even more than execution was being marooned alone on an island and left to die. This punishment was generally given only to traitors.

A Pirate's Life at Sea

Although piracy seemed to promise a life of wealth and freedom, life on board a pirate ship was, in fact, very difficult. Conditions were usually crowded, uncomfortable, and unsanitary. Seawater constantly leaked into the sleeping quarters. Every ship had rats. Always on the move to avoid naval ships, pirates often spent weeks at sea, where they faced storms and other dangers. Because of the hardships, few men engaged in piracy for more than a few years. Many died young from disease or battle injuries.

Because there was no way to refrigerate food on board ship, a pirate's diet usually consisted of biscuits and salt beef. The biscuits were often covered with mold, and the beef was full of worms and maggots. Rats often ate the food supplies. Without fresh fruit and vegetables, many seamen became sick from scurvy, a disease caused by a lack of vitamin C.

There were usually no doctors aboard pirate ships. The only medicines and medical instruments were those the pirates had stolen from other ships. The medical instruments were generally useless without doctors who knew how to use them. And the medicines of the time, usually made of herbs and other plants, were not very effective in treating sickness.

If a pirate or another sailor lost a leg, he was usually fitted with a wooden peg leg.

Pirate ships flew the Jolly Roger, a flag featuring a skull and crossed bones.

Without proper medical care, wounds easily became infected. Wounded limbs often required amputation. This procedure was usually done while the patient was drunk. Other pirates held him down, while someone sawed off the damaged limb. The wound was stitched up as well as possible and was covered with tar to prevent more bleeding. Many sailors, after losing a leg, would carve a peg leg from a piece of wood and attach it to the body with a leather strap.

In rough weather, everyone had to fight to keep from being washed overboard. Storms at sea could last several days. By the time the winds and rain lessened, most of the crew were exhausted, soaking wet, cold, bruised, and sometimes injured. Shipwrecks were frequent. Without modern radar, ships often got stuck on reefs, where waves could easily tear vessels apart. Sailors everywhere—pirates or otherwise—feared storms above any other danger. Many lost their lives in the swirling seas.

"Yo Ho Ho and a Bottle of Rum"

Most pirates had only one suit of clothes, which was seldom dry and nearly always dirty. Outfits varied from ship to ship, depending on the nationality of the crew. Those who had originally been naval seamen usually kept parts of their naval uniforms when they became pirates. The typical English pirate of the Golden Age wore a dark, loose-fitting jacket with bone or wooden buttons. He also wore breeches—knee-length trousers made of cotton cloth called calico. These pants were wide and comfortable for easy movement. A scarf or kerchief was tied around the head, while a wide sash was worn around the waist. Shoes were made of leather and had large buckles. Once on board ship, however, many pirates preferred to go barefoot for better footing on the slippery deck.

Much of the work that pirates (and all sailors) did was boring and repetitive. Every day, pirates had to climb up the ship's masts to handle the heavy canvas sails. Other crew members had to press strands of tarred rope between wooden planks to stop leaks. Damaged sails had to be repaired. Pumps had to be manned to keep seawater out of the ship.

Some seamen spent many lonely hours in the ship's crow's nest, a small platform one hundred feet above the deck. Using small telescopes called spyglasses, they watched for glimpses of land or approaching ships. Other sailors kept busy swabbing the deck, which basically involved mopping away the salt and dirt collected there.

To pass the time during their hours off duty, pirates played games of cards and dice. One of the most common pastimes was drinking rum. Alcoholism was widespread on pirate ships, and many men died as a result of drinking. Violent fights often broke out while men were intoxicated. Drunk and undisciplined, pirate crews were sometimes easy targets for attacks by warships or other groups of pirates.

Discipline was usually loose on pirate ships—drinking on the job was common.

Anne Bonny abandoned her women's clothing for a pirate's costume.

THE ADVENTURES OF ANNE BONNY

A number of pirates became famous during the Golden Age. One of the most famous was Anne Bonny. Anne and fellow pirate Mary Read are two of the most extraordinary female pirates in history. Charles Johnson wrote a great deal about their lives— although modern historians question whether Johnson's stories are entirely accurate.

Johnson tells us that Anne Bonny was born in Ireland in 1700 and moved with her parents to South Carolina as a young girl. The family lived on a small plantation near Charles Towne (modern Charleston). According to legend, it was in Charles Towne that Anne saw Blackbeard, the infamous pirate who captivated her.

Not long afterward, Johnson continues, Anne met James Bonny. He was a handsome young man. But what appealed to Anne most was that James was a sailor—and, even better, a pirate. Anne's father was furious when she told him that she wanted to marry James. Her father had already arranged for her to marry a neighboring medical student. That was the last thing in the world Anne wanted. She didn't want to spend the rest of her life in Charles Towne. She wanted adventure. Anne married James against her father's wishes. She followed him to the port of Nassau in the Bahamas.

Nassau was a beautiful place and a very busy port, with sailing ships of every kind in the harbor. It was also an ideal pirate haven. The harbor waters were

Even in modern times, Nassau is a busy seaport.

perfect for small pirate ships but too shallow for naval warships. The high hills surrounding the harbor gave pirates a good view of approaching enemy ships or potential victims. By 1710 Nassau was home to the largest settlement of pirates in the New World. An estimated 1,500 pirates made their headquarters there.

It was into this pirate stronghold that James Bonny and his new wife, Anne, arrived. Anne soon found herself bored and disappointed with her situation. James didn't want to be a pirate anymore, nor did he want anything to do with sailing. When James learned that the government was offering rewards to people who would turn in pirates, he decided to use his first-hand knowledge of piracy to earn money. He informed on his old pirate friends. Anne was furious and had nothing but contempt for his decision.

She began to spend less and less time at home. She hung out at pirate bars, and she soon met Captain Jack Rackham. Better known as Calico Jack because of the striped cotton pants he wore, Rackham was a well-known pirate with a gleam in his eye.

Jack noticed Anne immediately—many say he fell in love with her at first glance. Anne pleaded with Jack to take her away with him. But she was still married to James Bonny. She had asked for a divorce, but James had refused. James threatened to have Anne whipped if she didn't return to him. So Jack and Anne decided to run off together. They found a fast ship called the *Curlew,* which they plotted to steal.

PIRATE SHIPS AT SEA

Pirates of the Golden Age operated every kind of ship imaginable. Most often, they had little choice in the matter. They simply sailed whatever vessel they could capture. The single-masted sloop was common. This ship had one mast (tall pole to support sails) that could be rigged with many different arrangements of sails. Two-masted schooners were also widely used. These vessels were swift and easy to maneuver, even in small bays.

The biggest pirate vessel was the three-masted, square-rigged ship. It was usually more than sixty feet long and could hold up to two hundred people. The ship had square sails and was also equipped with long oars, so it could be rowed on days without wind. Three-masted ships could carry more cannons than other ships, making them a favorite with pirate captains.

Pirate captains and crews took great pride in their ships. They sailed under the Jolly Roger—a black flag showing a skull above crossed bones. Pirates also gave their vessels colorful names—the fiercer the better. Examples include *Revenger, Sudden Death, Flying Horse, Flying Dragon,* and *Holy Vengeance.*

In attacking another ship, the two most important tactics were surprise and speed. Pirate ships commonly hid in creeks or bays, then suddenly emerged into the path of unsuspecting victims. Another tactic was to find a merchant or naval ship at anchor and to creep up silently and attack at dawn. Yet another strategy was to disguise the pirate ship and crew as an ordinary merchant or naval outfit and to approach without causing suspicion.

Pirates preferred small ships that were fast and easy to handle during battles and getaways. These vessels frequently destroyed larger merchant ships.

Anne Bonny's sweetheart, Calico Jack

Anne casually strolled along the Nassau waterfront each day. She began to flirt with two young sailors who stood guard on the *Curlew*. The sailors were friendly in return. They told Anne important information about the ship, including what time the guard was changed at night.

The night that Jack and Anne chose for their mission was dark and rainy. Anne had learned from the two guards that most of the ship's crew members were on shore drinking. She and Jack crept silently on board the nearly deserted ship. Anne drew her sword and pistol and sneaked up behind the guards. Pointing a gun at their heads, she and Jack tied up the two men. Then the rest of Jack's pirate crew came aboard and sailed the ship quietly out of the harbor. Once they were safely at sea, Anne and Jack released the two prisoners, giving them a small boat with which to reach shore.

To conceal her identity, Anne disguised herself in men's clothing—a pair of black velvet trousers with polished silver coins along the outside seams. She cut her hair like the men and used the same weapons. She took her place beside the other sailors and fought as fiercely as they did. For the next six months, Calico Jack and his crew sailed the seas around the Bahamas. Attacking ship after ship, they had soon amassed quite a large fortune.

After a time at sea, Anne started to get sick to her stomach nearly every morning. She felt unsteady on her feet. She soon realized that she was pregnant. Jack suggested that they put aside their piracy for a brief time. The two sailed to Cuba, another safe haven for pirates and their families. Their baby, a girl, was born two months prematurely. She died within an hour of birth.

Anne and Jack returned to sea and their life of piracy. It wasn't long before they caught sight of a large two-masted ship. They made plans to overtake and board the vessel. Pirates quickly manned two large cannons on the *Curlew*'s deck. Other men rushed to the sails.

As the pirate ship came alongside the other vessel, Calico Jack raised the pirate flag—the skull and crossed bones. Shooting a cannonball in warning, the pirates stood on deck waving their pistols and swords. Within moments, the captain of the other ship appeared on deck holding a white flag of surrender. Without any bloodshed or injury, the pirates had captured yet another vessel—this one a Dutch ship.

The pirates swarmed onto the captured ship and took prisoners. Anne led a group of pirates down into the hold, where they found chests of fine silks and other valuables. These items would bring a high price back on shore.

As was common practice, the pirates persuaded many of the Dutch crewmen to join them in their quest for adventure and treasure. As the Dutch sailors took their places among the pirates, Anne's eyes fell

WEAPONS OF THE GOLDEN ERA

Flintlock **muskets and pistols** were common weapons during the Golden Age of Piracy, yet they were heavy, hard to use, and frequently inaccurate. Both kinds of guns required gunpowder, which pirates kept in a small leather flask with a metal lid. Musket balls (bullets) were made of lead. Wrapped in small patches of cloth, they had to be loaded one at a time.

Cannons were loaded in much the same manner as flintlock guns. Pirates loaded gunpowder, a plug of cloth or paper, and a ball through the cannon's muzzle, then lit a fuse. A single cannonball, weighing as much as twenty pounds, could do massive damage to an enemy ship.

Stinkpots were clay jars filled with sulfur. They were lit afire and then thrown onto opposing vessels. As with tear gas, the resulting smoke caused choking and tearing of the eyes.

Grenades were homemade devices. They consisted of pieces of metal and gunpowder crammed into old bottles, with fuses placed in the bottlenecks. When lit and thrown at the enemy, these weapons could do extensive damage.

Cutlasses were big swords with curved blades. Nearly a yard in length, these weapons were incredibly sharp and heavy. The sight of a pirate swinging a cutlass in the air could send fear through one and all.

Dirks were smaller knives used for fighting at close range. Long and thin, a dirk could easily pierce a human chest and enter the heart.

Axes, driven into the side of the ship, helped pirates climb aboard enemy vessels. Pirates also used axes to cut down the enemy's sails.

Grappling irons were hooks with four barbed points. Pirates used them to draw enemy ships close enough for boarding.

This variation of the Jolly Roger flag shows crossed swords rather than crossed bones.

on a handsome young sailor with blue eyes. Slender and well built, this sailor captured Anne's heart. She fell in love almost immediately.

One night when the moon was full, Anne managed to find the young sailor alone. Not at all shy, Anne told him that she had fallen in love with him. She revealed herself to be a woman and asked if the sailor could return her feelings. Anne was surprised when the young seaman began to laugh. She was even more shocked when he took the cap off his head and showed himself to be a woman of Anne's own age. Learning that the love of her life was a pretty young

Englishwoman named Mary Read, Anne began to laugh as well.

ANOTHER WOMAN ABOARD

Much of what we know about Mary Read also comes from Charles Johnson's book. Again, historians don't always agree with his fanciful version of Mary's adventures. Johnson explains that Mary went to sea as a teenager, disguised as a boy. He writes that Mary had "entered herself on board a Man of War [naval vessel], where she served some time."

She soon became bored and decided to try something different. She joined the army and "went over to Flanders [in Belgium] and carried arms . . . as a cadet. . . . She behaved herself with a great deal of bravery."

While serving in the army, Mary fell in love with another soldier and married him. The newlyweds settled down and opened a small tavern called the Three Horseshoes. Not long afterward, Mary's husband died of a fever, and the tavern failed. Determined not to sit around as a lonely widow, Mary became a sailor again. She shipped out on the Dutch vessel that Anne and Jack would later capture.

When Calico Jack saw Anne and Mary together, "he flew into a rage and threatened to cut [Anne's] new lover's throat." He quickly quieted down when Mary took off her cap and revealed the truth—that she was also a woman. Jack promised both young women that he would keep their female identity secret.

Anne's shipmate, Mary Read, also disguised herself in men's clothing.

Life returned to normal on the pirate ship as Anne, Mary, and the men went about their daily chores. Soon, Mary fell in love with Tom Deane, another sailor from the Dutch ship. She revealed her true gender to Tom. The two began to spend every moment together, but trouble soon developed. A quarrel broke out between Tom and a veteran pirate who had a reputation for fierce fighting.

The rules on a pirate ship were very clear. Any quarrel between the men had to be settled in a gentlemanly way. The two sailors would be set ashore at the first opportunity and would take part in a duel.

Fear swept through Mary. She knew Tom couldn't win the fight. Desperately, she gambled on her own fighting skills. She deliberately picked a fight with the old sailor and persuaded Calico Jack that her quarrel needed to be settled before Tom's.

Mary and the other pirate were put ashore, and their duel began. First they fired pistols, but both missed. Then they turned to their swords. The years Mary had spent in the military served her well. She fought fiercely. She waited for just the right moment to attack. Her opponent let his guard down for only one instant, but it was all that Mary needed. She thrust at him with her sword, and he fell dead at her feet. She had saved herself and the man she loved.

After her victory, Mary decided to do away with her disguise. She revealed herself as a woman to the whole crew. Since she had proven herself to be a good

Anne and Mary with their weapons at the ready

fighter, the other pirates accepted her without protest. Anne decided the time had come for her to tell the truth as well. The two women began to work on deck in long skirts with their hair hanging loose. When another vessel approached, however, Mary and Anne returned to their sailor's clothing. They continued to fight side by side with the men.

CAPTURE AND TRIAL

The king of England, as well as his governors, were fed up with piracy in the New World. In 1720 the governor of Jamaica hired a fast ship and crew and ordered them to set sail immediately. The governor wanted Calico Jack, and he would stop at nothing to capture him.

The ship's captain was Jonathan Barnett. Encouraged by the promise of a rich payment, Barnett set out on his mission. He soon found Jack's ship, but Jack and his crew were poorly prepared to fight. They had recently looted a ship, and most of them were celebrating their success. Many of Jack's pirates were passed out drunk on deck, while others were below deck still drinking. When Barnett fired a cannon shot in warning, many of the pirates simply jumped overboard.

As Barnett and his men boarded the vessel, Anne ran her sword through two of them. Turning around, she caught sight of Calico Jack and several other pirates scrambling down the ladder to hide below deck. Outraged, she screamed, "Dogs! If instead of these weaklings I only had some women with me."

Virtually alone, Mary and Anne fought bravely and courageously. Side by side, they slashed wildly with their swords, injuring some of their attackers. But the odds were against them, and soon they were forced to surrender.

Captain Barnett sailed back to Jamaica with his prisoners. Calico Jack, Anne, Mary, and the other pirates were put in irons and turned over to the governor. Charged with robberies, piracy, and other crimes, the pirates were brought to trial. Calico Jack and the male pirates were all found guilty and sentenced to hang. Anne was not particularly upset. She believed Jack deserved his punishment because of his cowardice in not fighting back.

Then came the trial of Anne and Mary. Witness after witness testified that the two women had been willing and active members of Jack's crew. The witnesses also attested to the women's use of violence. The women were found guilty. The judge asked if there were any reason why they should not be hanged. Anne stood before the court in her black velvet trousers. She looked at the judge and spoke calmly. "My Lord, we Plead our Bellies," she said.

That statement was the traditional plea of pregnant women of the time. It was against the law to kill an unborn child by executing the mother. In this way, Anne and Mary were saved from hanging. They were both sentenced to prison instead, although they were not really pregnant as they had claimed.

The prison was crowded and full of rats. The food was even worse than what the women had eaten on board ship. The cells were dark and wet. Many prisoners died of disease and starvation. Mary Read was one of them. She died of a violent fever soon after the trial.

Anne, however, mysteriously vanished from the official records. Many people believe that her father, who had business contacts in Jamaica, forgave his

RACHEL WALL

achel Wall, originally from Pennsylvania, worked as a pirate in the late 1700s. Rachel was married to George Wall, a young sailor who worked on a fishing boat. The two moved to Boston, where Rachel took a job as a maid in a rich household. George continued his fishing job. On one of his many leaves from sailing, George got so drunk that he missed his ship leaving port. He soon came up with a new idea for making money. "We'll be pirates and get rich!" he told Rachel.

Rachel was more than agreeable to this plan. The young couple borrowed a ship from a friend and went to sea. Faking a distress call, they lured a large merchant vessel close to them. Convincing the merchant sailors that they were harmless, the pirates wined and dined their victims. With the two ships anchored close to one another for the night, the drunken merchant sailors fell into bed. Just before dawn, George and Rachel boarded the other ship and killed the sleeping crew. Taking over the bigger ship, the Walls were well on their way to a life of piracy.

On a voyage a few months later, George was killed during a fight with another ship. Rachel immediately took command of their ship and sailed to safety. Not sure she wanted to continue pirating without her husband, Rachel returned to Boston and her old job as a maid. But by then, she had acquired a taste for riches and luxury.

Not long afterward, Rachel attacked a young woman wearing expensive clothing, hoping to steal her fancy bonnet. She was caught, tried, and convicted of robbery and assault. "I confess to having been a pirate," Rachel admitted boldly from the witness stand. "And I wouldn't mind being hanged for piracy but to be tried for robbery is degrading." A few days later, Rachel Wall was hanged.

daughter for running off to sea and bought her freedom. She then probably returned to the Carolinas, where she assumed a new name and a new life—at just twenty years of age.

WOMEN AT SEA

Anne and Mary's story raises many questions. Was it unusual for women to go to sea? Was it really possible for a woman to pass herself off as a man aboard a cramped and crowded pirate ship? Did Anne and Mary really live and fight among a crew of male pirates?

Actually, women who decided to dress and live as men were not unheard of in Mary and Anne's time. There were clear advantages to doing this. In the 1600s and 1700s, women did not have the same educational or financial opportunities that men did. Wives were considered inferior to their husbands. Usually, women could not move around freely without a male companion.

Most jobs, including sailing, were off limits to women in this era. So a woman who wanted the freedom and riches of a pirate's life usually had to disguise herself as a man. Some women, like Anne and Mary, did just that. Other women disguised themselves in military uniforms and became soldiers. Sometimes, injury forced them to reveal their true gender. Other times, their secrets were not discovered until death.

In Anne and Mary's time, women were thought to be too fragile for a life at sea.

By dressing as men, these women were taking a great risk. An English law passed in 1643 stated that "No woman shall falsify her sex by wearing a man's clothing. She subjects herself thusly to the strictest penalty that the Law or Our wrath may ordain." Similar laws were in place in other countries. Yet, like Anne and Mary, women sometimes found it worthwhile to take the risk.

DIFFERING OPINIONS

Historians agree that Anne and Mary really existed, but not all historians agree with the somewhat romantic version of their lives given by Charles Johnson. While Johnson describes Anne as a pretty redhead, modern scholars say she may actually have looked quite different. In fact, some sources report that she was a powerfully built woman who weighed more than two hundred pounds, stood over six feet tall, and was not pretty at all.

Modern sources also disagree with the story that Anne met Jack Rackham in a bar and then became a pirate. Researchers instead report that the two were serving together on a pirate ship when, led by Anne, the men mutinied. With Anne's support, the men voted Jack as their new captain. Anne became Jack's first mate but soon evicted him from the captain's quarters. She then assumed control of the pirate ship.

Whatever the truth, one thing is clear. Anne and

Mary thrived in this otherwise male world of pirates and desperadoes. They knew the risks and freely chose the danger. They chose to follow a violent dream. They both yearned for a life of adventure and excitement. As pirates, they certainly got what they hoped for.

Lady Ching was fierce in battle.

Chapter **FIVE**

THE PIRATE
EMPIRES OF
CHINA

ATLANTIC AND CARIBBEAN PIRACY CAME TO AN END,
for the most part, in the early 1700s, when Great
Britain began to crack down on piracy in the New
World. This was not true in Asia, where Chinese pirates
ruled the seas well into the twentieth century. But
piracy was different in Asia than it was in Europe and
the New World. Pirate ships did not operate indepen-
dently. Rather, large fleets of highly organized Chinese
ships sailed together. Piracy was a community business
with tens of thousands of pirates roaming the Chinese
coast. Many of these fleets were virtual empires—almost like nations at sea.

Whereas European and American women rarely became pirates, piracy was very much a family undertaking

in China. It was not at all unusual for women to work on pirate crews or even to command ships. These women fought with bravery beside the men, carrying cutlasses and other weapons. In fact, some of the most famous Chinese pirates were women.

"THE GREATEST PIRATE IN HISTORY"

Historians generally agree that Lady Ching was one of the greatest pirates—male or female—who ever lived. For more than three years, she controlled and operated one of the largest groups of pirates ever assembled. Many historians feel that Lady Ching may have been the greatest pirate ever.

Lady Ching's story begins around 1800 with Ching Yi, a Chinese man of considerable wealth. Most of his money came from his thriving pirate empire. Despite his immense wealth and power, Ching Yi was not happy. He was lonely and yearned to find a wife. He had courted many of China's finest young women, but none of them had suited him.

One day Ching Yi led an attack and captured a ship. When he learned that the vessel was carrying a group of Chinese prostitutes in addition to its expensive cargo, he had the women brought before him. His eyes were drawn to an exceptionally powerful and imposing woman.

He asked that she be brought to him. The woman, however, immediately leaped upon Ching Yi, nearly gouging out his eyes. The pirate captain was greatly

HELP FROM THE SPIRITS

According to historian Ulrike Klausmann, Lady Ching never made an important military decision without first consulting a guardian spirit. "Communication with the spirit world, especially the use of oracles—a kind of fortune teller—was and still is an important element of political as well as everyday life in China," Klausmann explains. For instance, no emperor ever married without first looking at the horoscope of his intended bride.

Lady Ching kept a likeness of her guardian spirit on each of the ships in her command. This spirit communicated with Lady Ching through dreams and meditation. She always obeyed its commands. When Lady Ching said that the spirit had given the order to attack, the fleet responded, even if the decision appeared to be irrational.

impressed by this woman's ferocity and beauty. He offered to marry her and was astounded when she refused. He offered her gold and riches, only to have her refuse again. Finally, Ching Yi asked what it would take for the woman to accept his proposal. Looking him straight in the eye, she asked for joint command of his vast fleet. Ching Yi readily agreed.

The two were married in 1801 and within four years had created a huge pirate empire. With fleets of junks and thousands of pirates, they dominated the coastal

Pirates flourished around China's busy seaports.

waters of southern China, attacking nearly every vessel that crossed their paths. They lived off the equipment and cargo that they captured at sea. When these supplies ran out, the pirates raided coastal villages. The two also ran a huge shakedown racket—collecting fees from merchants in exchange for not attacking their ships and for protecting them from other pirates.

When Ching Yi died in 1807, his wife moved quickly. After securing the support of many of her husband's relatives, she called a meeting of the pirate family to discuss who their new leader would be. Lady Ching was determined to take over the empire and made plans accordingly.

She was the last to arrive at the meeting, for she wanted to make a dramatic entrance. Wearing a robe of purple and blue, embroidered with gold dragons, Lady Ching dressed as her husband had. With her swords tucked into a wide sash, she placed his war helmet on her head and entered the room.

As Lady Ching faced the other members of the pirate empire, she quickly made her intentions clear: "Look at me Captains. Your departed chief sat in council with me. Your most powerful fleet . . . under my command took more prizes than any other. Do you think I will bow to any other chief?" Not one voice challenged her.

Lady Ching's first action was to appoint Chang Pao as commander of the Red Flag Fleet, the most powerful fleet in the empire. This was a very shrewd move. Chang Pao, a fisherman's son, had years earlier been captured by Ching Yi. The pirate leader had been so taken by the young man's courage and willingness to learn that he had formally adopted him. Over the years, Chang Pao had proved himself to be a loyal and brilliant son and great leader. Acting as commander in chief of the empire, Lady Ching put Chang Pao in charge of day-to-day operations. Within a few years, the two married to solidify the bond between them.

One of their first joint decisions was to institute a strict code of conduct that included harsh punishments for various offenses. The punishment for disobeying orders or stealing from the common treasury was beheading. The rules were equally strict concerning the treatment of women prisoners. Rape was forbidden and punishable by death.

Under Lady Ching and Chang Pao's combined leadership, the empire expanded. At the height of her power, Lady Ching's pirate fleet was larger than that of most country's navies. Her piracy was making sea travel dangerous. It also had a devastating effect on the Chinese economy. With little cargo reaching port, trade with Europe dropped to an all-time low.

Finally, in 1810, Chinese officials enlisted the help of English warships to rid the South China Sea of pirates. The English were only too willing to help—piracy in China had hurt their economy as well.

While a large force of Chinese and British warships

Chinese pirates attack a merchant ship.

CHINESE JUNKS

Chinese pirates and other sailors traditionally made their way across the seas in powerful wooden vessels called junks. Junks were about the same size as European merchant ships. They could carry as many as four hundred people and were usually fitted with twenty or thirty cannons. With their speed and agility, the vessels were nearly impossible to stop.

The origin of the junk is shrouded in legend. One story says that "Emperor Fu His, the child of a sea nymph, taught the Chinese how to build the craft." Italian explorer Marco Polo, who visited China in the 1200s, was very impressed with the junk. "[Junks] have a single deck . . . and have four masts with as many sails," Polo wrote. He felt the junk was far superior to any ship in his native Italy.

Chinese pirates protected their junks with an impressive collection of weapons. Most powerful of all were cannons that fired eighteen-pound balls with great accuracy. Chinese pirates also carried a weapon called a blunderbuss. It was a crudely built gun with a barrel nearly seven feet in length. The most deadly Chinese weapon, however, was the bamboo pike. It was a long pole with a sharp blade that was used in face-to-face combat.

Steam-powered gunboats were invented in the late 1800s. Wooden junks were no match for these faster, larger ships with their modern weapons. Eventually, military gunboat crews were able to defeat the Chinese pirates.

was being readied, the Chinese emperor offered a pardon to all pirates who surrendered peacefully. Lady Ching thought long and hard about this offer. She ultimately decided it was time to retire. She set out to secure the most favorable deal for herself and her pirate crew.

On April 18, 1810, Lady Ching, accompanied by a dozen or more women and children, boarded a government ship. Greeted with music and gun salutes, she was treated like the queen of a very powerful country. The government was willing to go to great lengths get Lady Ching to retire. It said her pirates could keep whatever goods they had stolen and plundered. It gave her a palace, high honors, and command of part of the imperial fleet. In exchange, Lady Ching and nearly 20,000 of her pirates agreed to surrender their junks and weapons.

A TWENTIETH-CENTURY PIRATE

By the mid-1800s, piracy had mostly died out in China. During the 1920s, however, China was torn apart by a great civil war. With the government in turmoil, piracy on the South China Sea once again flourished. Emerging to take control of yet another vast pirate empire was a small, innocent-looking woman named Lai Cho San. Her looks were deceiving—at heart she was a ruthless woman whose power and fortune were enormous.

At an early age, Lai Cho San had inherited her

father's criminal domain, which consisted of numerous gambling establishments and a small fleet of junks. She continued her father's shakedown racket, collecting large sums of money from merchants in exchange for protection, much as Lady Ching had done before her. Lai used the profits from this business to expand her pirating activities. She found piracy much to her liking and soon amassed enough money to recruit other Chinese pirates into her empire.

Increasingly, Lai's pirates were attacking European and American vessels. Aleko Lilius, an American journalist, was sent to China to investigate the situation. He tracked down Lai Cho San and received permission to sail on one of her ships. His reports have provided future generations with a close-up look at this famous pirate.

What Lilius discovered about Lai fascinated him. "The entire time I had the feeling of living side by side with a mystery," he wrote. On land, Lai always dressed in the finest garments. "Her usual costume was a white silk gown decorated with jade buttons," Lilius noted. Because of her refined appearance and charm, she was readily accepted into the homes of the rich and powerful. With her hair twisted in a knot and fastened with expensive jewelry, Lai certainly didn't look anything like a pirate.

The moment that she set foot on her ship, however, she became another person entirely. Kicking her sandals aside, she would stride across the deck barefoot. Soon

Lai Cho San led a powerful pirate empire.

she would change into simple men's clothing, complete with a gun that she could use quite accurately.

Lai Cho San was always accompanied by two maid-servants. These women delivered orders to the crew, for Lai never spoke directly to the men. In fact, male crew members were forbidden to enter her cabin. Despite her lack of interaction with the men, the entire fleet was quite loyal to Lai. Her orders were carried out without question, as raid after raid brought the money rolling in.

During her career, Lai led more than seven hundred raids against other vessels and coastal villages. She ran her fleet with an iron hand. Disobedience was severely punished, and the crew was required to obey a strict code of conduct. She did not spare hostages, either. For instance, if she did not receive a timely ransom payment for a kidnapped prisoner, she would order the prisoner's ear or finger cut off. She would then send the body part to the prisoner's family as a warning. If the ransom still wasn't paid, the hostage would be killed. Because of Lai's reputation, most ransoms were paid quickly.

Lai Cho San's last reported battle occurred in December 1937 during the Chinese–Japanese War. The Japanese were attacking any and all Chinese vessels in an attempt to gain land and power. Journalist Robert de la Croix described the scene: "On the one side there were Japanese torpedo boats of the modern sort . . . each equipped with six cannon. On the other side were . . . junks with strange sails. . . . [By the next day] not only did the entire [pirate] fleet now lie on the ocean floor, but its captain [Lai] had gone down with it."

Taking a stand for women's rights, modern-day "pirates" captured a ship in Cologne, Germany, which lies on the banks of the Rhine River, above.

EPILOGUE

IN THE FOOTSTEPS OF PIRATES

The year is 1990, and the place is Cologne, Germany, on the first day of the Rhineland Carnival. The festivities are in high gear along the harbor. An old and luxurious steamship, the *City of Cologne,* floats offshore. It has been anchored in the harbor for many years and is used to show important visitors around the city.

But on this festival day, the ship is about to serve another purpose. As the many festivalgoers continue their celebration, a cry goes up. A big group of wild-looking women suddenly appears. Wearing eye patches, they carry a Jolly Roger—the pirate flag. They're dressed as pirates and accompanied by children dressed as pirates. About two hundred women and children boldly board the old ship.

They take the ship hostage and demand more rights for women in Cologne. They condemn the city's housing shortage, which is particularly hard on low-income women. The women set forth their demands, including "spaces for women who discuss and work out their own goals and ideas and want to undertake their own initiatives." They demand that the ship be converted from a prestigious place into a cultural and communication center for women.

Negotiations with the city begin. Meanwhile, the women maintain control of the ship. More women come on board, bringing soup and sleeping bags. The pirates dance and drum on deck, waiting to see if their demands will be met. Six days pass, and no agreement is reached. The mayor of Cologne hints that he intends to have the ship cleared by force. By the next morning, the women have left the ship. They have simply disappeared.

Of course, these women weren't really pirates—not in the traditional sense. No treasure was taken. There was no violence—no one was killed or held hostage. And the ship was eventually returned to the city. But not before the women had expressed their demands for better living conditions and equal rights. Although these demands were not met, the women's bold actions and determination were both in the best tradition of piracy.

CARRYING ON THE TRADITION

Every culture includes nonconformists, people who refuse to abide by society's rules and norms. Over the years, many of these nonconformists have been women. Instead of the traditional roles of marriage and motherhood, these women have taken different paths. Some of them even became pirates.

These women were called mavericks, rebels, loners, misfits, and much worse. They often paid a price for their actions. Some of them were shunned or punished for refusing to follow society's rules. But in spite of opposition, they lived on their own terms. They had a zest for life and a need for adventure and excitement. They took matters into their own hands and set forth to discover the world for themselves.

The female pirates discussed in this book were definitely rebels and misfits. They all made names for themselves in the male-dominated world of piracy. Their deeds are all the more notable considering that most of them lived hundreds of years ago, before the modern women's rights movement.

Still, these women were criminals. They broke the law, and some of them were punished for their crimes. We might not admire their violent methods, but we can respect their courage and independent spirits.

SOURCES

10   Robert E. Lee, *Blackbeard the Pirate* (Winston-Salem, NC:
     John F. Blair, 1974), 21, quoting Charles Johnson, *The
     General History of the Robberies and Murders of the Most
     Notorious Pyrates*, edited by Arthur L. Haywood (1724;
     reprint, London: Routledge and Kegan Paul LTD, 1955).

29   Ulrike Klausmann, Marion Meinzerin, and Gabriel Kuhn,
     Women Pirates and the Politics of the Jolly Roger
     (Montreal: Black Rose Books, 1997),114.

31   *O'Malley*, n.d., <http://members.nbci.com/-
     XMCM/earlygen/htale1.html> (March 12, 2001).

37   *Granuaile*, n.d., <http://www.maths.tcd.ie/~haymin/-
     sca/Granuail.htm> (March 12, 2001).

39–40 Ibid.; 40–41 Ibid.

41   *O'Malley*, n.d., <http://members.nbci.com/-
     XMCM/earlygen/htale1.html> (March 12, 2001).

71   Charles Johnson, "A General History of the Pyrates,"
     Arthur Ransom Literary Pages, September 17, 1997,
     <http://www.arthur-ransom.org/ar/literary/pyrates.htm>
     (March 12, 2001).

71   Ibid.

71   Linda Grant De Pauw, *Seafaring Women* (Boston:
     Houghton Mifflin Company, 1982), 36, quoting Johnson.

75   *Welcome to the Domain of Anne Bonny*, n.d.,
     <http://www.geocities.com/CollegePark/4704/annebonny.
     html> (December 20, 2001).

76   Ibid.

77   Nancy Roberts, *Blackbeard and Other Pirates of the
     Atlantic Coast* (Winston-Salem, NC: John F. Blair, 1993),
     189.

77   Ibid., 197.

80   Klausmann, *Women Pirates*, 204.

85   Ibid., 41.

87   Jones, *Women Warriors*, 28.

90   Angus Konstam, *The History of Piracy* (New York: Lyon
     Press, 1999), 170.

90   Ibid.
92   Klausmann, *Women Pirates,* 56.
92   Jones, *Women Warriors,* 21.
94–95   Klausmann, *Women Pirates,* 58–59.
97   Ibid., 4.

GLOSSARY

desertion: abandoning one's job without permission

fleet: a group of ships operating under a single command

hull: the body of a ship

junk: a wooden Chinese ship with square sails

mast: a tall pole in the middle of a ship that is used to support the sails

musket: an early firearm that had to be loaded through the muzzle

mutiny: rebellion against an authority figure, such as a ship's caption

New World: another name for the Western Hemisphere, coined during the early years of European exploration and settlement there

press-gang: a group that tricks or kidnaps men on shore, forcing them into the navy

privateer: a private ship that attacks enemies with permission of the government

schooner: a ship with two or more masts

sloop: a single-masted ship

square-rigged: having square sails

stern: the rear of a ship

SELECTED BIBLIOGRAPHY

Botting, Douglas. *The Pirates*. Alexandria, VA: Time-Life Books, 1978.

Carse, Robert. *The Age of Piracy*. New York: Grosset and Dunlap, 1965.

Cordingly, David. *Pirates*. Atlanta: Turner Publications, 1996.

———. *Under the Black Flag*. New York: Random House, 1995.

De Pauw, Linda Grant. *Seafaring Women*. Boston: Houghton Mifflin Company, 1982.

Feder, Joshua B. *Pirates*. New York: Michael Friedman Publishing Group, 1996.

Graham-Campbell, James. *The Viking World*. New Haven, CT: Ticknor and Fields, 1980.

Jones, David E. *Women Warriors: A History*. Washington, DC: Brasseys, 1997.

Klausmann, Ulrike, Marion Meinzerin, and Gabriel Kuhn. *Women Pirates and the Politics of the Jolly Roger*. Montreal: Black Rose Books, 1997.

Klindt-Jensen, Ole. *The World of the Vikings*. Washington, DC: Robert B. Luce, Inc., 1970.

Konstam, Angus. *The History of Piracy*. New York: Lyon Press, 1999.

Lee, Robert E. *Blackbeard the Pirate*. Winston-Salem, NC: John F. Blair, 1974.

Magnusson, Magnus. *Hammer of the North: Myths and Heroes of the Viking Age*. New York: G. P. Putnam's Sons, 1976.

Rankin, Hugh F. *The Pirates of Colonial North Carolina*. Raleigh, NC: North Carolina Department of Cultural Resources, 1996.

Roberts, Nancy. *Blackbeard and Other Pirates of the Atlantic Coast*. Winston-Salem, NC: John F. Blair, 1993.

Rogozinski, Jan. *Pirates, Brigands, Buccaneers and Privateers in Fact, Fiction and Legend*. New York: Facts on File, 1995.

Sherry, Frank. *Raiders and Rebels*. New York: St. Martin's Press, 1986.

FOR FURTHER READING

Black, Clinton. *Pirates of the West Indies.* New York: Cambridge University Press, 1989.

Exquemelin, A. O. *Exquemelin and the Pirates of the Caribbean.* Edited by Jane Shuter. Austin, TX: Raintree/Steck Vaughn, 1995.

Hawes, Charles Boardman. *The Dark Frigate.* New York: Little Brown & Co., 1996.

Meltzer, Milton. *Piracy and Plunder: A Murderous Business.* New York: Dutton Books, 2001.

Stevenson, Robert Louis. *Treasure Island.* 1883. Reprint, New York: Atheneum, 1981.

Weatherly, Myra. *Women Pirates: Eight Stories of Adventure.* Greensboro, NC: Morgan Reynolds, 1998.

MUSEUMS WITH PIRATE AND SEAFARING EXHIBITS

Mariner's Museum

Visitors to this museum will find loads of information about seafaring life, including a special exhibit about women and the sea.

Mariner's Museum
100 Museum Drive
Newport News, VA 23606
<http://www.mariner.org>

Maritime Museum of the Atlantic

The museum offers a wealth of information about naval and merchant ships, shipwrecks, shipbuilding, and life at sea.

Maritime Museum of the Atlantic
1675 Lower Water Street
Halifax, Nova Scotia
Canada B3J 1S3
<http://www.maritimemuseum.gov.ns.ca/mma/>

Mystic Seaport

Visitors will see a bustling nineteenth-century village of tall ships and historic buildings, exhibit halls brimming with seafaring artifacts and images, and a unique shipyard where the nearly lost art of wooden shipbuilding endures.

Mystic Seaport
The Museum of America and the Sea
75 Greenmanville Avenue
Mystic, CT 06355
<http://www.mysticseaport.org>

The New England Pirate Museum

Here you can board a full-length pirate ship, learn all about pirate life, and view sunken ships and pirate treasures.

The New England Pirate Museum
274 Derby Street
Salem, MA 01970
<http://www.piratemuseum.com/pirate/pirate.htm>

Teach's Hole

This exhibit features a life-size replica of Blackbeard in full battle dress, along with displays of pirate-era weapons, maps, coins, flags, and more.

Teach's Hole
Blackbeard Exhibit and Pyrate Specialty Shoppe
P.O. Box 276
Ocracoke, NC 27960
<http://www.teachshole.com>

PIRATE MUSIC

Music was an essential part of pirate life, both to lift the spirits of the crew and to inspire them in battle. Popular instruments were squeezeboxes (accordions) and fiddles. Most pirate shanties, or songs, were rather bawdy and spoke of pirate exploits. This ballad, originally printed on a large sheet of paper called a broadside, tells about the adventures of a female pirate.

The Female Smuggler
(From *Sea Songs and Shanties,* collected by Captain W. B. Whall. 1910. Reprint, Glasgow, Scotland: Brown, Son & Ferguson, Ltd. Publishers, 1974.)

> O come list a while, and you shall hear,
> By the rolling sea lived a maiden fair.
> Her father had followed the smuggling trade,
> Like a warlike hero.
> Like a warlike hero that never was afraid.
>
> Now, in sailor's clothing young Jane did go,
> Dressed like a sailor from top to toe
> Her aged father was the only care
> Of this female smuggler.
> Of this female smuggler who never did despair.
>
> With her pistols loaded she went aboard.
> And by her side hung a glittering sword,

In her belt two daggers; well armed for war
Was this female smuggler,
Was this female smuggler, who never feared a
    scar.

Now they had not sail-ed far from the land,
When a strange sail brought them to a stand.
"These are sea robbers," this maid did cry,
But the female smuggler,
But the female smuggler will conquer or will die.

Alongside, then, this strange vessel came.
"Cheer up," cried Jane, "we will board the same;
We'll run all chances to rise or fall,"
Cried this female smuggler,
Cried this female smuggler, who never feared a
    ball.

Now they killed those pirates and took their
    store,
And soon returned to old Eng-a-land's shore.
With a keg of brandy she walked along,
Did this female smuggler,
Did this female smuggler, and sweetly sang a
    song.

Now they were followed by the blockade,
Who in irons strong did put this fair maid.
But when they brought her for to be ter-ied,

This young female smuggler,
This young female smuggler stood dress-ed like a
    bride.

Their commodore against her appeared,
And for her life she did greatly fear.
When he did find to his great surprise
'Twas a female smuggler,
'Twas a female smuggler had fought him in
    disguise.

He to the judge and the jury said,
"I cannot prosecute this maid,
Pardon for her on my knees I crave,
For this female smuggler,
For this female smuggler so valiant and so
    brave."

Then this commodore to her father went,
To gain her hand he asked his consent.
His consent he gained, so the commodore
And the female smuggler,
And the female smuggler are one for evermore.

INDEX

OTHER TITLES FROM LERNER AND A&E®:

Arthur Ashe

The Beatles

Benjamin Franklin

Bill Gates

Bruce Lee

Carl Sagan

Chief Crazy Horse

Christopher Reeve

Edgar Allan Poe

Eleanor Roosevelt

George W. Bush

George Lucas

Gloria Estefan

Jack London

Jacques Cousteau

Jane Austen

Jesse Owens

Jesse Ventura

Jimi Hendrix

John Glenn

Latin Sensations

Legends of Dracula

Legends of Santa Claus

Louisa May Alcott

Madeleine Albright

Malcolm X

Mark Twain

Maya Angelou

Mohandas Gandhi

Mother Teresa

Nelson Mandela

Oprah Winfrey

Princess Diana

Queen Cleopatra

Queen Elizabeth I

Queen Latifah

Rosie O'Donnell

Saint Joan of Arc

Thurgood Marshall

Tiger Woods

William Shakespeare

Wilma Rudolph

Women in Space

Women of the Wild West

ABOUT THE AUTHOR

Anne Wallace Sharp has written magazine articles and books for young readers. She has also written articles and a book for adults. Her interests include reading, traveling, and spending time with her two grandchildren, Jacob and Nicole. She lives in Beavercreek, Ohio.

PHOTO ACKNOWLEDGMENTS

The images in this book are used with the permission of: Courtesy of © The Mariners' Museum, Newport News, Virginia, pp. 2, 9, 20, 55, 74; © Corbis, p. 6; © The Granger Collection, New York, pp. 14, 56, 66, 70; © Hulton Getty/Archive Photos, pp. 11, 60, 72, 79; The Art Archive/Garrick Club, p. 13; © Bettmann/Corbis, pp. 17, 34, 52; © National Maritime Museum, Greenwich, London, p. 18; © North Wind Picture Archives, pp. 23, 59, 89, 90; © Hulton-Deutsch Collection/Corbis, pp. 26-7; © Carmen Redondo/Corbis, p. 29; Courtesy of the National Library of Ireland, p. 30; © Gustavo Tomsich/Corbis, p. 33; © Art Resource, NY, p. 38; Ulrike Klausmann, *Women Pirates and the Politics of the Jolly Roger*, New York 1997, p. 44; © Fine Art Photographic Library, London/Art Resource, NY, p. 48; The Library of Congress, p. 51 (LC-B8171-4016); © Galen Rowell/Corbis, p. 62; © Christie's Images/Corbis, pp. 64-65; Philip Gosse, *The History of Piracy*, New York 1932, p. 82; © Peabody Museum of Salem, p. 86 (#1518); Ulrike Ottinger, *Madame X, Eine Absolute Herrsherin*, Frankfort 1979, p. 93; © Felix Zaska/Corbis, p. 96.

Front Cover, Courtesy of © The Mariners' Museum, Newport News, Virginia. Back Cover, © North Wind Picture Archives

All attempts were made to contact the copyright owner. If an image appears without credit, please contact Lerner Publishing Group.